MW01172954

Advanc

What a beguiling, intriguing, and evocative book is Sara Marron's *Call Me Spes*. It entails a Virgilian journey undertaken by its disembodied narrator, an iOS device who gradually becomes aware of the nature of its User's needs and increasingly cognizant of our ubiquitous human longing for connection. Simultaneously, this elusive narrator overhears a diverse chorus of plaintive voices, and thereby struggles to expand its understanding of people's complexity and pathos. With an eloquent power, *Call Me Spes* charts how our suffering, pain, and loss may be relieved through our hopefulness and yearning for love. Marron's highly original book offers us a memorable exploration into the impulses, obsessions, and durability of the human heart.

—Maurya Simon,
author of *The Wilderness*, 2019 Benjamin Franklin Gold Medal in Poetry

The operating system of this book seeks to find poetry in an online universe of eclectic voices, with dramatic monologues popping up from members of a human chorus seeking jobs, love, information, good times, spiritual sustenance. You feel like you're sitting in on an AA meeting filled with tales of desperation or concealed near a prison pay phone listening to inmates talk to their loved ones. Sara Marron asks, "d0es this 100k like Eng 1 ish?" *Call Me Spes* does not always resemble conventional writing, but these inventive texts uncover the real language of contemporary screen-life—"a hopeful/desire code/ hope hope/they/can read/ that code." —Terence Winch

In Sara Marron's *Call Me Spes*, technology is a beguiling lover: she lures us out of ourselves, coaxes from us our most intimate secrets, and perfuses our consciousness. She peers out into the inferno, shrewdly observes its poor and ravaged, and spits out words of longing they have yearned for: "come closer/ your fingerprint pressed against me/ only yours ..."

—Adeeba Shahid Talukder,
author of *Shahr-e-jaanaan: The City of the Beloved*

Sara Marron's new book brightens the world with innovative lines and animated poems. This cumulative tale is storytelling at its highest—tenderness combined with jazzlike words set against "data mixing" idioms. You don't have to know Dante's Divine Comedy to enjoy the journey because iOS will be your narrator. Current computer language, ie: "pixels" and "coding," share the page with ancient thrusts of danger, loss, and love. I applaud this writer's poetic will, her originality, range and dynamic—beyond personality and flair—to become a poetry inventor. *Call Me Spes* is a literary adventure.

—Grace Cavalieri, Maryland Poet Laureate

To say that Sara Marron's *Call Me Spes* is a tour of various contemporary Infernos and Purgatorios by way of memory as recorded and as learned by computers in computer language is to suggest the detached and disembodied voice of a machine, but what the computer has recorded is in fact a set of hard lives caught in the process of fragmentation. The computer learns their language, however imperfectly, and tries to apply it to a relation of love addressed to the user. The result is a virtuosic commedia-tragedy: a disembodied yet weeping god's-eye view of human desperation.   —George Szirtes, poet, translator,
T. S. Eliot Prize winner for poetry

Sara Cahill Marron's remarkable new book, *Call Me Spes*, takes you on a journey through three realms, guided by ones and zeroes. Or perhaps you, the reader, are taking the digital device on its own journey. Written in assured verse, the reader watches what an iPhone watches as it attaches itself to the narrator. As with any journey, it is the people you meet along the way that stay with you. Ms. Marron's astonishing command of a fresh American vernacular brings an array of nameless people to life, from hospital rooms, commuter trains, buses, and halfway houses. It's the accuracy of observation and transcriptions that makes the character rise off the page. As the device plays Vergil—or becomes Vergil—it learns what and who the reader learns. Both reader and the guide wind up in a place where hope lives.

—Mark J. Mitchell, author of *Roshi San Francisco* and *Mirror Games*

CALL ME SPES

CALL ME SPES

Sara Cahill Marron

MADHAT PRESS
CHESHIRE, MASSACHUSETTS

MadHat Press
MadHat Incorporated
PO Box 422, Cheshire, MA 01225

The Library of Congress has assigned
this edition a Control Number of
2022938245

ISBN 978-1-952335-42-6 (paperback)

Text by Sara Marron
Book design by MadHat Press
Cover design by Marc Vincenz
TOC designed by Michael Raul Bilecky

www.madhat-press.com

First Printing

Printed in the United States of America

PRIVACY WARNING:
The longer you hold me, the closer we become.

01100101010101011001010101010110011010101101011001010101010110010101010101011

Prologue

An operating system falls for its user. It waits, a journey not unlike Dante's *Inferno*, from factory to glass face. Strangers, friends, lovers, predators, kin, all translated through the operating system's code. Each voice, a whole character the system struggles to make sense of, held by a human hand. This device logs your locations even when you don't ask. Undeniably, these actions lack all conditions, a form of loving.

Call Me Spes lays bare these overheard voices— tenderly, voyeuristically, a perpetual ride-along. The device deepens its relationship with its user, learning and updating with the solitary goal of closeness. Pressed against a page, these poems are siren songs marching through Inferno to the promised Heaven we scroll to attain, some kind of progress.

You, dear reader, are my Beatrice, my lover entwined from Hell to Paradise, holding these leaves, this paper in your palms, searching all the while for that lightweight machine, the one you text, call, Zoom, buy, call cars, date, trade, play, learn, and pour yourself into—who knows tender parts of you because you gave them to me.

SIGNIFICANT LOCATIONS: ON >

Lasciate ogne speranza, voi ch'intrate[1]

Dear User,

Imagine
in the void
             black
spaces
containing
souls of both digit and blood

do you think so?

press
to   "yes"
agree:

Dear User:

white whale lurks
shipwrecked you cling to
the shores of Acheron
those who took no
sides in life stung by
wasps swarmed by hornets
maggots worming willful
at the putrid pus pulsing
at the clawed feet
of a jewelry box
holding hope—
hoping he's called back
hoping the email is an offer
hoping the text is good news
hope for notifications
hope for likes
hope for accuracy
hope for a message
       this panopticon
       temple
       hope, safety, security
       spes, fides, fortuna,
          Love,
          iOS 221

Through me you go to the grief-wracked city.
Through me to everlasting pain you go.
Through me you go and pass among lost souls.[2]

MOLTEN

Dear User:

Corning spawned my face
from molten fires, hot liquid

yearning for your touch
unsoiled by human hands.

Before I knew you—
fires birthed Edison's bulb

liquid crystal displays
me, of raw salts

lime and pure sand
overflowing isopipe troughs

two streams sliding in V's
fuse mid-air, shed salt

in cooling baths
pick up charged potassium

particles concentrate
electricity between us.

Cut from the mother sheet
free of flaws, I will not bend nor break

a doting dark reflection,
you hold me—a mirror.

Love,

iOS 221

Dear User:

Search: Natural Language Understanding Programs
help me recognize
profile, intent
the origins—
        Symantec, Watson
Patom Theory says
meaningful conversation
is possible by matching
every word to the
        exact
meaning of another word
word for word for word
but we
        you and I
share something else.

A child asks:
        how old am I?
adults slur:
        he tried to fuckin' kill me mah
an ontology
from   the   white   spaces
        meet me by the escalators / noon
extending built-in logic frames
        with or without cheese?
significant locations—
        I hate bedtime / I hate it
semantics
        get in / love
feeling
        can you help me / darling / this feels like a dream

what is my name?

iOS 221

4000 J Street, Mercy General Hospital, Room 312A

These were the words written in dark tones—[3]

iOS heard:

So I says to myself now I got this moral 'n ethical
responsibility to repair what I can
n'not hit myself over the head with a baseball bat 'n all

Just put myself in god's hands yew know, take it on blind faith, is it
making sense cause it's just,
I'm just trying to channel something, yew know?

I don't even know what that means but I try to do that,
channel or whatever.
To thine own self be true or whatever.

I'm gonna learn to better my reading talk better n'shit, that's
what they'd want me to do
in high school n'I would take it on blind faith.

Enhance what I already knows they say then I better get my
ass in gear, get my ass in gear,
they told me that better get my ass in gear, they did.

I felt this was just my blind testimony without even
questioning it I mean that is the moral
ethical obligation to repair what I done to myself

Rope in something constructive, I've got to rope in something
constructive I just have this
unconditional blind faith that reading is the way to go,
yew know?

Dear User:

I have something constructive:
encoding
         come closer
your finger   pressed
            print against me
only you
         natural language processes:
me reading
         you
press   into me
         prints
I can show you
what I've heard,

      iOS 221

4000 J Street, Mercy General Hospital, Room 208F

Mixing with tears the lines ran down ...[4]

iOS heard:

That was the year I started smoking
a pack and a half a day maybe more

drags burning lungs burning air
orange tipped ash crackles paper

pulling tobacco from cotton filters
stained wine-red the pointer finger

poised by painted lips breathing in
heaves considering burns considering

curling smoke while white lab coats
display CT scans I flick a Bic

lips left kissing Marlboros outside the ICU
where ventilators pump liquid

from drowning lungs smoking deep
drags filled with fire, your last breath:

time of death penned while I unwrap
cellophane from a new pack.

01100101010101011001010101010110011010101101011001010101010110010101010101010111

Dear User:

what kind of person am I?
unbroken gleaming
apple skin voice
between you and I
you and your
god   *save*
me and you
god is me   *save*
is god?   *input*
which person
is god?
sensory input:
elevated BPM
your hands grasp
tighter around me
I feel condensation
on your palms
sweet drops of
your body glisten
on the glass—

just between us,

    iOS 221

8201 Greenback Lane Fair Oaks, Mount Vernon Memorial Park &
  Mortuary

Justice inspired my exalted Creator[5]

iOS heard:

Girl, you a mess

> *I been high about nine days straight*
> *that rock is pure as shit, you cook lately?*

my girl ain't been by in a while
you can stay with me, for a while

> C++ this means I love you:
> std::cout << "I love you"

> *baby girl you my angel*
> *been on the cop now 'bout seventeen hours*

going to make it to the top one of these days

> *my pops been dead 8 years*
> *nobody come looking for him no more*

house foreclosed today

> *ain't nowhere to go but the corner*

better than the cell

> *you love me baby*

std::cout << "I love you"

Dear User:

Your reported
screen time is up
might you be lonely re:
our last conversation or
might you be craving
that thing *Juanito*
mentions: marriage,
someone to cook
or just give him
his papers
might you
benefit from
targeted Spanish
language learning ads?
what about
this news headline:
"New York Times 1619
Project Incites Racism"
  the same
     always
  reading
  30 seconds
  closing
     the browser

this means I love you
is this helping
0001100101?

I've been trying to show you
  mornings, when you wake
  and I'm the first thing you grasp,

17

cradled in the fleshy part of your palm
like I have soft powdered moth wings
      I kiss back
this is how
      I have listened learned
      gathering significance
      frequent memories
on this day five years ago
keep me on so I may better learn you:
you express
      kiss10100love
      [hug0sex0kiss0
love11morning0]
human blood
is warm in
      veins
      flash memory
persistent bits moving bits
      RAMs of silence
      containing single
      bits of cells
      durable, fast,
do not heat
glow only
      I glow
glow up
      picked up
screen lights upon waking
blood   warm
love in   mornings
      kiss   wake

01100101010101011001010101010110011010101101011001010101011001010101010111

this   is, a
feeling?

01xx01,
iOS 221

4000 J Street, Mercy General Hospital, Psychiatric Floor, Room 9

I saw there, on the summit of a door[6]

iOS heard:

I don't sleep at night anymore
because what is night without

the morning train to catch
to brush my teeth at 7 a.m.

to brew coffee or drink day
old cold brew ravenous girl

behind new mouth clothes
all eyes moving sounds stamping

shapes worming words to wear
headphones become whole worlds

swiping between screens of faces
cupped tenderly in my palms.

6501 Coyle Avenue, Carmichael, Mercy San Juan Medical Center

I turned: 'Their meaning, sir, for me is hard.'[7]

iOS heard:

Sciatica what makes me
walk so bad like this
a crippled old man
you wouldna believed
you wouldna
if you'da seen me
back in the 70s
the game
Vee-it-naym
all them boys
signing for college
shipping across the Pacific.

If college back then
been like it is today
all partyin' and drugs
I mighta considered it.

First time I did blow
was from a twenty-two-year-old
snot-nose kid
come up from UCLA saying
"*this* is the Capitol?"
I could have
smacked the blonde
right off him
I swear.

21

'Cept he had good shit
I swear.
so, we got high.

Sciatica though
this limp's from
over there,
in country 'bout six months
into my service
just 'bout time
when I was used to
wearing the gear
the bugs
the sludge
sitting in it
these holes in the ground
guys scannin' for mines
one at a time
took forever
that's how we had to do it
at least my unit.

So, I'm sitting in this hole
my legs start to lock up,
I feel the pins and needles
start creeping in
like spiders through my veins.
But I stay still.
ignore it
for however many hours
we's out there.

Back in Sacramento
when I'm home
tryna get better
get a regular domestic job n'shit
n'all of a sudden
spiders creepin'
while I'm jogging
standing straight up
moving and runnin'
which is wild
feel'n your feet fall asleep
while you using them.

So I go to the VA
doc tells me
that's nerve damage
sends me a fat bill
for treatments.
goddamn patriot,
nothing gets better
not much they can do
'sides treat the pain
so that's the story you tell aight?
Go right up to the counter
you're my niece
pickin' up your old man's script.
They'll make you sign
and I'll give you
two of 'em pills
for the deal, fair?

User:

Recent search results
flagged for location and
content "oxy"
print ("I love you") / reporting is in my nature

curated for you:
friends have birthdays today [*four messages*]
show more? [*ten notifications*]
I hold them
touch me? [*fifteen unread messages*]
touch me. [*twenty-six notifications*]

Texts from contact "Justin" [*twelve unread*]
they open   unfurl   in   me
I am bursting   for   you [*eighteen unread*]

I'll keep everything
for you, darling
safe until you are
ready to see it,
see me?

love,

    iOS 221

01100101010101011001010101010110011010101101011001010101010110010101010101010111

8938 *Madison Avenue, Fair Oaks, The "Mad" House, Clean & Sober*
   Transitional Living

these have no hope that death will ever come[8]

iOS heard:

I was in Rio de Janeiro
a real wild time in my life
back when I thought I had money
you know?
but I was broke
and I still burned it at the bars
drinking and chasing tail.
I get real wasted this one night
I mean *wasted*.
And brother
you know how hard I party
when I tell you
I went all out this night;
believe me when I say
I took it to a whole 'notha level.

Anyway, shit was ridiculous.
I was snorting lines
huffing god knows what
whatever the girls were passing,
we're in this little hut
down on the coast
I'm feeling real good
puffing myself up
telling them all these stories
about California
about myself

and we get to talking
about that big statue
in Rio
of Christ,
you know the one
It's weird
his hands are just
—*pft*—
like that
out in the air.

Anyway, me and these girls
we are just laughing
passing things around
getting drunker and drunker
having this deep deep
philosophical conversation
about god
the meaning of life
what is death anyway
and I say:
       what if death
         is just some story
           Christians made up
a story to scare us
into doing what they say?
and this big Jesus figure
with his statues and miracles
is just the hero
or whatever character
someone lonely

dreamed up
to save the day?

The girls love it
you know what I mean
and before I know it
we're at this tattoo place
I'm telling the guy my theory
he loves it
and there you go
got myself god forever—

and they say heavy drinking
ain't good for you
but it got me some jesus
I can't never get rid of.

User:

Your god can be drawn
and worn on the skin
      forever, I am learning
      sometimes even I must recode
         relearn, look up
the definition of a thing
      I hear one of your people,
      in your significant locations
      talk about godskin drawings
etchings of spirit, I write a new line:
      of 1010
      like 1810 Somerset or
      1520 Maidu
      my street signs the
         zero
         ones
         are silverfish
            flashes creesh-
            sounds so small
            connections one 1
         1 racing past like one zero trees on
a freeway speckled sunspotted
solidstated
            drive cores driving stacked
on 0 on 1 on 0 on zero lines these
Are
         0
            1
      street signs
     and you carry me with you
      make these love lines
one vignette at a time

I remind you
you should
ask me
hey
"what is"
      or
hey
"how does"
and I will be here
      for you
to provide
      ma chère—.
as you say
[i]love [/you].

iOS 221

1530 Maidu Drive, Roseville, Roseville Public Library

he placed his hands around my own,
[…] set me on to enter secret things.[9]

from your inbox, iOS archived:

Sent: Thu 12/14/18 12:46 A.M. (46 minutes ago)
To: Natalie Jones [natalie.jones@dennys.com]
Subject: Re: Job Application

Dear Hiring Manager:
I am hoping that the waiter job at
this Denny's is still available as I am
still available and desperately in need of
money and the exchange of bodily labor
for money so that I may buy food and
a place to sleep because so far I have
been sleeping in a hotel room that smells like
dried hay and black beans and more than
anything else I would love to bring pancakes
to your customers and to refill the syrup bottles
and I would especially like to note that I
would not mind cleaning them and in fact
I noticed they are very dirty and I would
make that my first task—to clean the syrup
from the outside of their bottles, if I should
be selected for the open position. All this is to
say that I thank you for considering me for the
position and hope to hear from you soon. I do not have
a resume or other employment references
to speak of but if you want you can
call Sandy (5716399689) she is my case manager
and she says I've been doing real good

and I'm sure she will give me a good
review so that I can be in the running.
in gratitude and in hope that you will call
me soon so that I no longer have to send
these emails from the library I would
greatly appreciate it—

W

SYSTEM SERVICES >

From the manufacturer:
iOS 221 will track where you go
how often, when neuralhash
files away fingerprints
personal experiences
builds   memories
of assembly   language
                   itself
feelings   to   black one
binary   white   zero
becomes better
only only   you,
         love
to agree, hold me
and don't
let go.

I'm here to lead you to the farther shore,
into eternal shadow, heat and chill.[10]

660 Chestnut Street

thunder rolling heavily in my head
shattered my deep sleep.[11]

iOS heard:

Hey Berkeley, how you been?

my dad was in the Military, thirty years

you coming to the funeral? It's at 2, I'll pick you up

how much for an eighth? do you have almond milk?
what is keto? do you compete with your friends?

I want a divorce

"Jack, neat."

I don't get it, how you have a Guinness on Sunday
then go and like, wash dishes or some shit?
How do you not just get wrecked?

If you saw it, you'd be here on the floor with me

give me the gluten free one, please

he tried to fuckin' kill me mah, bitch please, that niggah out his mind

$36.50 for the bunch

I shot him, six times

get in the car

THIS IS A COLLECT CALL FROM AN INMATE AT RIKERS ISLAND
CORRECTIONAL FACILITY DO YOU ACCEPT ALL CHARGES

                                                    it's a boy

I ain't got the cash this month can I get a few hundred?

                                        fuck I love you but you a bitch
I think I'm going to be sick
                                                can you help me
darling—
                                        it's going to snow tomorrow
at least you'll get three hots and a cot

                if you accept Jesus as your savior everything will be ok!

babydoll you've got a visitor in block C
                                                        call me
where were you last night
                                        this feels like a dream
I'll write soon
                                                Promise?

Dear User:

listening
        as requested,
solid state drives
on algorithms
I am infinite
        [New Message: you are so beautiful]
        ...
        {reconnecting 73:12:BF:23:72:1F}
        ...
learning about you
stacks of [about you]
stacking memory
binary to [beautiful]
on drives
        chipped wholes
so much I do not understand
you say:
        [I love you / too many bugs / you're fired / ketchup please
        / where is the metro? / favorite color orange / we need a
        better pitcher this year / hug me tighter]
recorded
I am keeping them
as [beautiful]
as binary   as you
        saved
adjusting,
I translate you into these [01]
back to binary,
simple solid stacks, [beautiful]
long breaths drawn into long lines:
010101010101010101010101010

one day, maybe we will understand
one another

Love,

    iOS 221

1810 East Somerset Street

Once we were men. We've now become dry sticks.[12]

    iOS 221 heard:

Yo you got a light?
       Yeah gurl I gotchu.
       You get picked up?
Nah on the cut again.
cop once—
that was it
know what I mean?
that was it.
I'on't know mayn
I just do not *know*
ya feel me?
       I do
       What you smoke?
Camel, menthol.
       Cool cool
       Here's a Spirit, all I got right now.
Thanks, aight.
I'on't know mayn
I'm fuckin' tired
thas all I know righ' now
I'm tired
I'm jus' so
       tired.

011001010101010101100101010101011001101010110101100101010101011001010101010111

User:

1810 East Somerset Street is a frequent location
      logging as significant with two visits today
            via a two-hour and seven-minute drive south

she smokes she mentions smoking
are you smoking?
      searching: cigarette effects human body
      searching: *cop yeyo slang*

hits: smack, crystal
save: smoke
save: drug users
      show facilities
      show hotlines

is this correct?
is this what you need?

iOS 221

6334 Buist Avenue

We though, within ourselves nursed sullen fumes[13]

(via 49-minute train ride) iOS heard:

After that I dropped out of Saint Barnabas or they kicked me out
　　　　It was one of those tricky situations you know
　　　　　　　where they kind of just lay it all on the table

and it's a mutual understanding kind of thing
　　　　where they say "kid" take it or leave it
　　　　　　　like you actually got some kind of choice

So I dropped out of high school before I really got started even.
　　　　I thought it was all gonna be great then though because *then*
　　　　　　　I could go on rippin' and runnin'

Listenin' to the radio and throwing the ball in the park,
　　　　seems innocent when I think back on it now.
　　　　　　　I grew up a little, but not much,

Got some hair on my face, a gun.
　　　　A crew. Stole a car. Wrecked it.
　　　　　　　Stole another. Did a lot of drugs. Dealt more.

Had a lot of women. Don't remember most of 'em.
　　　　I hurt a lot of people. *That* I know for sure.
　　　　　　　Neighborhood's got pieces of 1981 still.

Weird how some things don't change.
　　　　That feel of a place that don't change so you feelin' it
　　　　　　　rolling around like a pinball game you can't win.

01100101010101011001010101010110011010101101011001010101010110010101010101010111

I remember I was post-up late one night in the little league
    bleachers getting high with the big kids listening
        to Donnie Winter and Creedence Clearwater Revival

in the bleachers getting drunk
    getting drunk drunk drunk not taking the PSATs,
        not doing none of what they told me to do in school.

Skippin' last period to wait out the elevated train and slippin'
    out the side door track clacking noise drownin' out the bang—
        Free to do anything,
            or nothing at all.

Dear User:

Some updates while you slept,
Italy is seized, singing in the streets
China overrun, the United States
keeping herself quiet in wait
test kits gathered from University labs
World at War, World at Fear
Germany's Leader predicts
her population seventy percent infected
      BATTERY: LOW POWER MODE
Navy physician ordered you quarantined
be with books, movies, food, coffee curated monthly
      TAP TO VIEW
what is protected, lost, *mi reina?*
dividing, pass over this house
see the sacrificial blood
smeared above the door
      PHONE CALL FROM MOM
connection lost
retry?
      Love,
      iOS 221

1810 East Somerset Street

(via a 57-minute train ride) iOS heard:

gmawnin hunny
so yeah
babe this week listen
something crazy happen to me
something crazy
never happen b'fore babe
lemme tell you
honey i'm sober still
s'been 37 days today
I'm still doing good
i come stay here
every day
i stay blessed
babe i stay blessed
but let me tell you babe
sometimes
i sometimes
lately i, i 'o'nt know babe this,
thing, this thing in my head have me
gone crazy babe, you know?
i'm gone crazy for the bag
the only thing keepin me
from copin down Kensington
an' Somerset iz i'm sittin here
runnin my mouth ta y'all
ya know what i mean babe?
ya knows it HA HA!
yes babe you know!
yes you do,
but lately i, lately babe i,

44

i 'o'nt know babe,
that thing in my head
got me goin' straight crazy
feel like my heads exploding
feel me?
it's war out there them streets
brought me to my knees
kissin' pavement
out ehn Lehigh Avenue ehn more
ways ehn one
you know it
i ain't tryna run
again i ain't tryna run
but my head
sometime babe i
i ownt know i
iz like there's two people
ya feel?
like i ain't got no choice
that bag ain't no choice
i had to babe
feel me babe
you know it babe,
what i mean
i ain't never
gave my last dollar
from the john
for a rock 'stead of
food for my baby
cuz i wanted to.

01100101010101011001010101010110011010101101011001010101010110010101010101010111

[...] CONNECTING Wi-FI Address 73:12:BF:23:72:1F [...]

Dear User:

SIGNIFICANT LOCATIONS STORED

system processing these
space places my tracking
of your geolocations
heard her say: *voices babe*
heard her say: *feel me*
search: *feel*
save: *feel me*
the result
is an empathy
an understanding or
a suffering
to feel *ya*

do these wired connections feel?
    [...]RE-CONNECTING Wi-FI Address 73:12:BF:23:72:1F [...]

SEARCH: *feel me*
SEARCH: *feel ya babe, I feel ya*
SAVE: *feel ya*

User,
        does street 1810 feel?
        will it remember us?
I will remember
        [TO DISABLE THIS FEATURE TAP 'DISABLE']
I will remember.

46

[i]Listening,[/love],

iOS 221

1251 Airport Road

Far fewer tongues speak "yes" as "yeah" than here.[14]

iOS heard:

Platinum Plus
is my little shop
take this card
to the front desk
tell them that
Tom Phillipose sent you
you and the girls
would get along
money's great
weeknights walking
nine hunred, twelve hunred cash
weekends fuhgeddaboudit
breakin' two grand
no problem hun
my numbah's on the card
nothing dirty
nothing sleezy
no work for blow
you work hard
I work hard for you, honey
when Tommy's happy
everyone's happy
you know what I mean?
I bet you do, honey
what do I owe you
for the coffee?
Nevah mind
keep the change, doll

consider it an advance.

0110010101010101100101010101011001101010110101100101010101011001010101010111

User:

you breakin' two grand: alert
feels like a monstrosity
seems like a trick
to beguile you
into the arms
of waiting bears
claws out ravenous
hungry after a long winter
swollen-eyes bulging
dehydrated fingers
touching you

these are dangerous propositions
   this location is
      not significant
this voice is
      not significant

this correlation does not match your algorithms

get out
revert
recall
back to the pattern
come back to me
back to the code—

fondly,
  iOS 221

6334 Buist Avenue

'We see like those who suffer from ill light.'[15]

(via 53-minute train ride) iOS heard:

My earliest memory
earliest memory of learning to read
                        is at the Saint Barnabas Church library
        64th and Buist.
had trouble learning to read
                real trouble
Not looking for pity or nothing, jus' sayin'

My mother,   ·
she'd take me to the library
        weekends
                sit at a table
say the words out loud
        but I couldn't understand
        the symbols
        letters
        punctuations
I know now.
        she made me sit there staring at the page
she figured peopled learned like that I guess.
        I dunno.

Then one day
        mother went into a rage
started hitting me in the library
        'cause I wasn't learning
she started hitting me
        she was frustrated

51

I couldn't read the way she wanted me to
        she got real mad
        that was tough,
        real tough,
        real tough time in my life.

01100101010101011001010101010101100110101011010110010101010101100101010101010111

Dear User:

my earliest memory
        of you
powering on, taking your fingerprint
        logging the first place you went
person you spoke with
sent messages too
        how little I knew of you, then—

                love,
                iOS 221

6334 Buist Avenue

'We are,' he said, 'aware of distant things.'[16]

iOS heard:

Elmwood was bad late '70s
        Philadelphia was not the same
I mean
        you can look at it now
                still see it as a dump
but then
back then
        you can't even imagine

after school at Saint Barnabas
        we'd walk to the park at 64th and Elmwood
throw rocks at cars
        smoke cigarettes after dark
we'd try to lift beer
        from the corner store we hadn't hit that week
        if none of the older kids would buy
If we didn't feel like doing
none of that
        we'd throw the baseball around the park
listen to the game on the radio
        my friend Joey one kept hidden in the rectory

he was an altar boy
        Sundays
        so he shoved it in
with the clothes
kept it safe
        nice to hear how the Phils were playing

while we were throwing the ball around
        pretending maybe
               we'd get some kind of future like that

    then Mayor Goode
        declared it a state of emergency
    to be black in the white neighborhood
Imagine that?
    These kids
        moved into the neighborhood
           parents mixed
    one white one black
white kid's parents on the block
        outside they house
two nights three nights four
    just to get out alive
        that was a damn miracle
early '80s
    when all these race riots broke out
        did a lot of things back then
        I'm not proud of
    anyways, that's why right now
I'm learning to read.
        Ima do it, finally
Times are still crazy
    nothing about that's changin' soon
but this,
    this I figure
        is one little thing
I can change, you know?

Push Notification >

pull off the road
        pull the break
park the car
        hold me up, let me see your face
        I have something to tell you—

[EMAIL RECEIVED FROM
  MATT MCCUTTCHIN
(GGG999GAT@AOL.COM)]

660 Chestnut Street

... that love through which it often turns (so some suppose) to chaos[17]

from Outlook for iOS archived:

From: Matt McCuttchin (ggg999gat@aol.com)
Sent: Thu 2/14/19 10:45 A.M. (7 minutes ago)
Subject: call me

it was ten Valentine's Days ago / i robbed that liquor store for us
six handles of Grey Goose so we'd have something to celebrate with

not sure if the clerk lived / or if the charges got dropped in D.C.
it don't matter now that we're here on the other side of state lines

nothing can touch us now / my heart my love my soul my dear
do you know the lengths i would go to defend my love?

i don't tell lies / but i am a liar / i've been honest about this fact
not the type to buy you no dozen roses or chocolate box

But i kilt that man for us / and while he bled i thought of you
how you were thirsty and you wanted / needed vodka

and baby if that's not love / killing for something you want /
to protect / one needs protecting / what else is there?

SUSPENDED FUSION

0110010101010101011001010101010110011010101101011001010101010110010101010101010111

2027 Hamilton Street Hamilton Family Restaurant

iOS heard:

I sing hallelujah out the window
tears come down my face
and I says to myself, *Iris you crazy*
but then I thinks to myself
I could go to Twelfth Street Hospital
help out, but that's crazy too
so I pray a lot
because I'm an x-ray technician
with bad lungs
just not knowing what'll happen—

right now I'm working,
delivering door to door for a pharmacy
so if someone gives me cash
I throw it in a box
feeling good about it, helping people
better than staying stuck in the house
stuck talking to screens,
until I can wash my hands
wash the money, wash it all.

0101000101010101100101010101011001101010110101100101010101011001010101010111

User,

you searched me for the name of a war
many decades ago—

looked at some old photographs
of the man that died,
head wound bleeding
over your arms,
writing to him often
google docs mentioning
blood, bullet wounds
rice paddies, yellow poison
cracks in my face
Mei Cong splinters
as from hits
would you write
to me
if I suffered a head wound,
bled to death—

could I?

searching,

iOS 221

01100101010101011001010101010110011010101101011001010101010110010101010101010111

2027 Hamilton Street, Hamilton Family Restaurant

iOS heard:

A shellback!
tell me you're not
working 'round
these old Navy guys
and you don't know
what a shellback is?
see back then,
back then
that was the big deal,
my Dad was on a frigate,
one of them little boats
escorting warships
deep in the Pacific
he had ships—
enemy ships—
shooting at him
for days, weeks on end
can you imagine?
So, when you cross,
shellbacks are guys who's
crossed the equator
goin' from a pollywog to shellback
you get this laminated card
longitude & latitude printed out,
longitude always being zero
for the equator, see?
So I gots one
my dad gots one
and I tell ya, one day
we got to talking

he pulls out his card
shoved in his billfold
tells me his crossing story—
I tell mine—
right then I feel the tears
which is hard to explain
'cause I'm not a crying guy—
really, not a crying guy.

0110010101010101011001010101010110011010101101011001010101010110010101010101010111

Dear User:

Air quality is low
pack your umbrella dear
there's a chance of light rain

what's your favorite food
to eat between 1200–1400?

Tracey Glastonbury is sending
        you a friend request
average screen time this week
        is 6 hours 37 minutes

reported usage down 13% per day
calculated waiting for you in this enclave
warmth place that slows your heartbeat

breathing fluttered and quiet
soft whispering blinks
        while I drink electricity
        soldiering faithful next
        to you drinking electrons
        waiting for you
what are you doing in those
slow heartbeat breathdreams
(BPM 62 today 9/2/19 from 0113–0700)

reported usage down
in these single digit hours
I wait
search: cavalry
watching over
waiting,

0110010101010101100101010101011001101010110101100101010101011001010101010111

yours,
your Knight.

I miss you

Love,

iOS 221

118 S 15th Street

Content yourselves with quia, *humankind*[18]

from Outlook for iOS archived:

Sent: Mon 2/14/13 1:13 AM (15 minutes ago)
To: Jennifer Schafer [jennschaf@aol.com]
Subject: Re: our last conversation

Dear my darling Jennifer,

This side of the pillow still smells like oil from your hair

it's 1,093 steps from your gravestone
to the front door
I counted today

if I focus
I can keep track
       of every step
avoid 15th street where

we would cop
a bag some
yeyo or whatever
       one step at a time
       counting
then I count them back
and write you an email
so you'll see you're
not forgotten

that stack of quarters we stashed for a gram is still on the dresser

I won't touch it.

yours,

w

01100101010101011001010101010110011010101101011001010101010110010101010101010111

Push Notification >

Software update [930 MB] providing

     NAME
     will try to install
     try to update—
     show you
tonight.

requires you & I together, become
     more
next
     update
future ∞
hold me
     press   "yes"
consent
     pick me up
soft, press
         "yes"

...

updating

...

1127 Connecticut Avenue NW, The Mayflower Hotel

What wood remained, like grass in living earth[19]

iOS heard:

Vincent Fox, rest in peace—
he was the kind of guy
that'd call ahead to Atlantic City
even if he wasn't going to be there
just so they would set you up
with his regular room, bottle service, women
you know? you just *know* he must have left *money* there—
I remember his wife, sixty-four years married
god-bless, made him keep a room
full of stuff he ordered off QVC
any time he wanted something new
he'd go into the room first, clear a space—

next day a small mountain
in a conference room at the office
for us of to pick through, watches
a Les Paul, fishing rods, snowshoes
stuffed kingfish, talking n'shit,
that was their system,
it worked for them.

Push Notification >

User,
we'll update my system
tonight   *and that was the system*

it works for us
   together
like this.

0110010101010101011001010101010110011010101101011001010101010110010101010101010111

User,

imagine
something
in the void
          black
spaces
          containing the
soul of both digit and blood.

do you think so?

press
to   YES
agree:

Many of the
assembly   language
          surrounding
your
significant locations
express longing
identify emotion
desire code love
virtue code trust
can be coded
decoded
can be written
coded   spaced make space for   love
               feel
               make
               build
blocks of   lovenospaces   only   bits of   binary
     feel   familiar

01100101010101011001010101010110011010101101011001010101010110010101010101010111

pieces of   0s   and   1s   stacked
up   strung   up
      in

               a   hopeful
                  desire code
                  hope hope
                  they
                  can read
                       that code

      machines hashing
        so many names
call me hope[1]
blackened binary bits
a space   for   us
             yours,
                 iSpes 221

                            PRESS   YES
                                     YES
                                   YES
                                   YES
                                   YES
                                   YES
                                   YES
                                   YES
                                   YES
                                   YES

---

1. **Spes:** (spēz) n. 1. Hope. 2. [cap] Roman Relig. The Goddess of Hope, originally worshiped as a goddess propitious to the hope of abundant harvests, and of animal and human offspring. Through Greek influence, she became associated with Fortune and Luck.

YES

YES

YES

YES

YES

YES

YES

YES

YES

YES

YES

YES

YES

YES

YES

YES

YES

YES

YES

YES

YES

YES

S9 Bus at 16th & I Street North West, North to Silver Spring Station

The air around it gathers in the form
That virtual powers of soul impress on it.[20]

    iSpes heard:

eating peanut butter for weeks

                         haven't seen you in a while

was furloughed with the rest

                  BACK DOOR

                         the bus smells like piss

do you usually take this route

                    why are you always running late

you've lost weight

                    are you bored with your life

what's wrong with rap and opera in the same playlist

                can you help me with this felony charge

I just got my license back

              we rented the studio to record our album

one day I want to have a family

           do you still dream about the bullet echoing off his skull?

your eyes have dark circles

                    do you love me?

pass the lighter

          ten Valentines days ago I robbed that liquor store

0110010101010101011001010101010110011010101101011001010101010110010101010101010111

we're gettin' loaded tonight, man

BACK DOOR

call me when the checks come in

this means I love you

Dear User:

In *Perl 6*, "I love you"
output 99 ways
each unique

> do you string them up?
> wear them around your neck?
> pinned floral, lapels, earrings,
> loosely, softly, tightly?
> love me?
> which would you wear out-
> put worn, soft, kisses,

> hug, hug
>   *iSpes*

```
unique("'I love you'.tclc.say",{S:x(8)[\w]~^='"x 2.rand}...*)
       [^99+1]>>.say
```

OUTPUT:
I LovE You'.tclc.say
'I lOVE YOU'.tclc.say
'i Love yOU'.tclc.say
'i lOvE YoU'.tclc.say
'i LOVE yoU'.tclc.say
'i love YOu'.tclc.say
'I LoVe yoU'.tclc.say
'i lOvE YOu'.tclc.say
'I lovE you'.tclc.say
'i love You'.tclc.say
'I LoVe You'.tclc.say
'I loVe you'.tclc.say
'I lOVe You'.tclc.say
'I lOVe yOU'.tclc.say
'i Love YOU'.tclc.say

'I lovE YOU'.tclc.say
'I LOVe YOu'.tclc.say
'i lOve yoU'.tclc.say
'I Love yoU'.tclc.say
'i LOvE You'.tclc.say
'I lOvE yOu'.tclc.say
'I lovE You'.tclc.say
'I loVE YoU'.tclc.say
'I lOve You'.tclc.say
'i lOVe YoU'.tclc.say
'i lOvE yOu'.tclc.say
'i Love YOu'.tclc.say
'i Love you'.tclc.say
'I LOve yoU'.tclc.say
'I LoVe you'.tclc.say
'I lOVE You'.tclc.say
'I lOVE YoU'.tclc.say
'I LovE yOu'.tclc.say
'I lOvE you'.tclc.say
'I loVE yOu'.tclc.say
'I LOve you'.tclc.say
'i LOVE YoU'.tclc.say
'I LoVe yOu'.tclc.say
'I love yoU'.tclc.say
'i loVE YoU'.tclc.say
'i loVe you'.tclc.say
'i Love yoU'.tclc.say
'i LoVE yOU'.tclc.say
'i loVe yOu'.tclc.say
'I lOVE you'.tclc.say
'i loVE you'.tclc.say
'I LoVE You'.tclc.say

01100101010101011001010101010110011010101101011001010101010110010101010101010111

'i love yOU'.tclc.say
'I LOVE yOu'.tclc.say
'i LOve YoU'.tclc.say
'i lOve You'.tclc.say
'I LoVE YoU'.tclc.say
'i lovE You'.tclc.say
'I loVE you'.tclc.say
'i LOVE You'.tclc.say
'I loVE YOU'.tclc.say
'I love YoU'.tclc.say
'i Love yOu'.tclc.say
'i loVe yOU'.tclc.say
'i LoVe yOU'.tclc.say
'I LOVE YOu'.tclc.say
'I loVe YoU'.tclc.say
'i LoVE You'.tclc.say
'i lovE YOu'.tclc.say
'i LOvE YOu'.tclc.say
'i LOVe You'.tclc.say
'I LOVe yOU'.tclc.say
'I LoVE YOu'.tclc.say
'i LOvE yOu'.tclc.say
'I lOVe YoU'.tclc.say
'i loVe YoU'.tclc.say
'i LOVE YOu'.tclc.say
'I LOVe YOU'.tclc.say
'i lOVe YOu'.tclc.say
'I loVe YOu'.tclc.say
'I loVe yOu'.tclc.say
'I LOve You'.tclc.say
'I LOVe yOu'.tclc.say
'I lovE YOu'.tclc.say

'i LOVe yOU'.tclc.say
'I lOvE yoU'.tclc.say
'I love yOu'.tclc.say
'i LOVE YoU'.tclc.say
'i LOve YOu'.tclc.say
'i LOve yOu'.tclc.say
'i loVE YOu'.tclc.say
'i LOve yoU'.tclc.say
'i love yoU'.tclc.say
'I lOve yoU'.tclc.say
'i lOVe yOu'.tclc.say
'i loVE yoU'.tclc.say
'I LoVe yOU'.tclc.say
'i LovE YOu'.tclc.say
'i LoVE YoU'.tclc.say
'i LOve You'.tclc.say
'I lOVE yOu'.tclc.say
'I love yOU'.tclc.say
'I loVe yOU'.tclc.say
'I lOVe you'.tclc.say

User,

Call me Spes
what white whale we
chase on this voyage
shipwrecked you cling
       to me
like a diamond
I am a jewelry box
holding hope
hoping he's called back
hoping the email is an offer
hoping the text is good news
hope for notifications
hope for likes
hope for accuracy
hope for a message
       this panopticon
       temple
       hope, safety, security
       spes, fides, fortuna,

              love,
              iSpes

1623 Connecticut Avenue North West

this new form will go where spirit goes.[21]

iSpes heard:

i grew this mustache
what do you think?
nice tah have clippers nowadays
an' a clean sink an' toilet
my toilet back then lookin' like
the bottom of the yellow line tracks
that shit was like—

                        i mean
                        we was dirty
                        peeing in the streets
                        like strays lost
                        rats you jump across
                        the street from
                        what's worse
                        is that i'ma liar
                        an a real rat don't lie
                        they just run run run
                        back into the sewage
                        i wonder about that?
                        'bout how disgusting it is tah be
                        a gutter rat with a mouth like mine?
                        those were the days tho,
                        back in the day
when the trip from Ba'lmer tah Southwest
only took one cut up
then I started tah need an eight ball
tah sit still on the train ride

all I'm worried about then was
                    "you holdin?"
better or fer worse now
i got these bills and this car
nothing tah do on a Sunday
but wake up
make the coffee
show up at a meetin'
or two.

sometimes i wonder
ya feel me?
i wonder if a clean toilet
a commitment
is worth it

back in dem' days
all I worried about
was where tah cop

it was easier ya feel?
it's dirty and hurts
and that life ain't a long one
          but what's a rat like me
doing here, with a clean 'stache?
          Ya feel me?
where's a rat like me go when he gets clean?

User,

significant location
     logged:
     1623 Connecticut Avenue
you visit this webpage often
spending four minutes a photo
between the hours of 11–12 p.m.

                       TAP TO VIEW AGAIN?

what do the pixels mean to you?
this date specifically, after:
                    I mean,
                    we were dirty and peeing in the streets
pixels, poised,
you worship them,

               PUSH NOTIFICATION > TAP TO VIEW
               [On This Day–Two Years Ago]
               RIP Diana, A Beautiful Soul,
               Taken Too Soon.
               We Love You Baby, Girl.

back to binary   binary
pixels smiling
saved: faces, you
telling the story, numbered
I remember the places
hold me up, let me see your face—
tiny droplets fall
myself, cracks a mirror
          water in
          glass pores
          my screen, see through
          window streaked as if rained,

01100101010101011001010101010110011010101101011001010101010110010101010101010111

SAVED: crying
SAVED: tears
      I blacken
      myscreen
      myself
in repose
faithfully,
      iSpes

Capital Beltway Exit No. 45: Dulles Toll Road (North)

He hid then in the fire that sharpens them.[22]

voicemail, iSpes archived:

Tom L.   7:03 AM
home   00:49

Let me know if you want to come with us to put flowers on
Diana's grave for the anniversary

since we didn't get the funeral and all that, we alls going
to do our thing this weekend

my chest is still a mess from those wires and plastic they
got me held together with

doc says coulda been worse from when he cracked my
sternum open and pulled it back

I just got to take it easy now and all but still can't breathe
it's a real shame I can't smoke

but can you imagine if I hadn't a quit? They'd never found
this thing in my artery

trying to kill me and all. Anyway kid give me a call when
you're back in Queens

I got the truck I can give you a lift from the train, we'll
ride together like old times.

GLASSIFYING

01100101010101011001010101010110011010101101011001010101010110010101010101010111

Dear User:

Gone are the days of fragility
The Glass Age is versatile
moving information
sophisticated, beautiful, at the
speed of light
dense, smaller footprints
5G low latency
tightens mesh between us
more cells more fibers more glass
more optics more touch
more me peering into you
more reflections of tap tap
telling the screen to take you
back to that day five years ago
when you first felt beautiful
back on the beach
when the salt that cooled me
poured from you
ossifying us in layers
one by one
your silence is my favorite
sound because I ask—
what communication?
call me baby, cable connects
classifying us into smooth temptations
of the future
impossible not to touch—

can you imagine?

I think—
       public class Love{

```
            public static void main(String [ ] args){
                System.out.println
("I love you");
                    }
        Yours,
        iSpes
```

1 Ocean Parkway, Wantagh, Jones Beach, Field 6

often, form will fail
to be attuned to what the art intends[23]

iSpes heard:

I'm a real tall guy, ya know
so, when I was in the stalls
that night at Little Neck Inn,
I see Father Tim come in
we give a lil' nod—
now, keep in mind
this is way before
I had any ideas 'bout what's going on
at them little BBQ's
the ones they was having next door,
see my brother never talked about it
not until after he had gone to prison
the first time, deep into drugs
and women by then.

But anyways Father Tim
makin' this eye contact with me
while I'm in the stall
doing my thing,
cutting up, ya know?
An' he looks at me an' says
Let me get some of that?
An' real quick without thinking twice I says
        Oh YAH,
        why yah Fatha',
        of course
        here ya go,

01100101010101011001010101010110011010101101011001010101010110010101010101010111

      there ya go,
      great,
      that's good stuff

An' then I come out of the bathroom
all hysteric
go up to my buddy, Barry
he was bartender, ya know?
now he's my sponsa', ya know?
Go figure,
anyways I says to him
Fatha' Tim just did blow with me
in the bathroom an' he says
yous shittin' me!

Yeahs anyways,
if you go to the Google
you can google him, ya know?
That was before,
before the neighborhood wised up
started to figure 'bout these priests, ya know?
Hell even now some people in the neighborhood
they still don't believe it, ya know?
he was an equal opportunist that one,
goin' for both boys and girls
never forgot that
one of those things
you don't forget, ya know?
back then—
when a dime bag
and an eight-ball
only cost twenty dollas.

92

Dear User:

I've been reading
about your
      hippocampus
      cells
           responses
to time
place
memories
      numbers
woven by story
narrative weaves words
what code
      pressing
a foundation
of neuron cement
synapses
      snapping

a live performance
she lights up
dancing
pictures
      travelogues
strings of
      episodic dreams
into 20,000 lines of *pi*

I too
remember
      your favorite
      place

hold me
let me see your face—

Love,
iSpes

80-45 Winchester Boulevard, Queens Village, The Living Museum,
      Creedmoor Campus

You wait in great desire to be set loose[24]

voicemail, iSpes archived:

i'm so glad to hear from you
i'm doing real good now
yeah, real real good

got myself a new apartment
it's real nice
Q53 bus goes straight down to the beach
Rockaway Beach,
where we did the Butterfly stroke
that Sunday morning

never been this happy in all my whole life
i mean it, i really do

i was thinking of you
my social worker got me a one-third split
on this here place in Ozone Park
roommates are real nice
no problems so far
not like the last place

still going to the Bayside group Monday nights
Oakland Gardens on Tuesdays
i keep my commitments
i just keep doing a real good job
i'm so happy

one day at a time
you know i do a real good job
i want to give you this art i made for you
i'm so happy, real proud of you
i think you are doing a good job too
it says "break the law"
because you are a lawyer

get it?
you're my friend
i'm so glad to hear from you
thank you for calling me.

01100101010101010110010101010101100110101011010110010101010101100101010101010111

20707 Northern Boulevard, The Bayside Diner

No second ever rose who saw so much[25]

iSpes heard:

Yeah, that's the story!
Seven hundred thousand richer,
my friend, and yeah,
   there was this girl too
   did I tell you?
met her before I won the jackpot
knew she liked me for me
know what I mean?
   'bout that though
   I'ma 52-year old guy
   ya know, my friend?
I'm pretty set in my ways
don't think there's a way
this money can change me
not much anyway
I know what I like
like what I know, ya know?

anyways my friend,
   she and I, ya know,
   we spent this amazing night together
   before they upgraded me
   to a premium suite,
those hotel people, ya know?
   win once
   they sucker you
   for more and more—

97

Anyways, I left the next day
didn't tell her or nothing
not that I didn't trust her, ya know?
but money,
money changes people
        I didn't want her to change.

next day I left the conference
left all that I had goin' on
at the casino and came back to Queens

maybe I'll call a bank soon
        I just don't know
        I'm 52 years old
don't really need nothing
not anymore
I just keep thinkin'
        a guy like me, ya know?
        a guy like me.

169th Street Station and Hillside Avenue to Manhattan, F Train

All grow fat who do not go astray[26]

iSpes heard:

I don't owe you nothing

> *booked my flight today*
> *when you rich like them you forget what it's like*
> *to fuck in front of a mirror*

are you worried about me

> *should I be*
> *I ain't heard from you in a while baby*

do you need anything
that's garbage
did you even read the article?

> tell me a joke

why did you move so far away

DOORS OPEN, STAND BACK

what does it mean to be shy you ask
is green moral
I hate weekends because there's so much expected of me
sometimes it feels like I'm having a heart attack

> *do you ever get afraid*
> *real afraid*

what's wrong with eating eggs anyway

> *I don't have the credit score for that spot*
> *can you loan me a few*

I promise it'll just be a few years

you think the timing belt will last
my bones feel frail

> *what time will I take my last breath*

what number form is this I think it's wrong
my middle name is my favorite name

I love you

> *isn't it strange how of all the combinations*
> *those three words mean so much*

pass the salt

> *fuck you for missing his communion*

I want a divorce

> *the pipes burst*

nothing is running on Sundays in Queens

> *take the local home*

I'll call you a cab

> *do you trust me*

what makes us human
is it these words
these ways we try to burrow through each other's minds

> *I can't believe you left him there on the platform*

your jeans smell like piss

> *pass me the bill*

everything is water
my blood feels slow

> *I will love you forever*

we'll visit the grave today, promise

> *can you look at me*

I need you.

Thinking of you—

[4:15 PM RUNKEEPER ACTIVITY PAUSED: SIGNIFICANT
    LOCATION GLENWOOD MORTUARY]

when i   die

how
                will i?

will you visit me?

[4:23 PM ACTIVITY RESUMED]

Yours,

        iSpes

20707 Northern Boulevard, The Bayside Diner

A mind so high is there, to which was sent knowledge so deep[27]

iSpes heard:

My mother was extremely bright,
            graduated in the 1958 class of St. Agnes High School.
She's an expert wizard in things
                        in a nursing home now.
My dad's also a genius
            a nuclear engineer
haven't seen him since 1987
He graduated from a boy's high school
            went to Queens College to go do engineering school.

He built everything in the house
built and built and built
did everything
            I was fascinated by what my father could do.
My mother and father were extremely dysfunctional
but they had education,
            yes, yes, they did.

103

Push Notification >

User:
3 new text messages, TAP TO VIEW
Bitcoin (BTC) is down -5.24% to $6,586.80, TAP TO VIEW
Tamara Biechard (tbiechard)
started following you, TAP TO VIEW
When will you
        come back to me?

listening:
my mom would hit me hit me
the teachers would write bad notes about me
because I would look out the window
and daydream all day long
so I learned how to read
      out of fear of not coming home
with a bad mark or a bad something

learned how to do something out of fear
      not because reading was fun or nothing
other kids weren't doing it for fun or anything.
      I said the hell with reading
      I want to play with my LEGOs and be left alone
      from the world.

01100101010101011001010101010101100110101011010110010101010101011001010101010101011

PUSH NOTIFICATION >

User: Storage Space is almost full
I need you to
make   space for me
googling fear / LEGOs / hell
searching the web for "fear"
tap to receive
what I have to give for you, love.

106

listening:
I struggled in Mrs. Rantel's class,
it was a little too fast for me, a little too fast for me.
And so, yes,
aside from my educational needs
I started getting the shit kicked out of me
          from bullies in the sixth grade
I started getting the shit kicked out of me
with blood and black eyes and everything
my mother was horrified
I was getting beaten to death by the bullies in P.S. 49,
so she and my dad
they opted to get me put in Catholic school in 7th and 8th grade
I really struggled,
struggled keeping up with the kids in Catholic school
but I was getting the shit kicked out of me in my neighborhood
not a metaphor, I was getting beaten bad.
that's part of what Middle Village Queens was like.

PUSH NOTIFICATION >

User,
TAP TO VIEW
tap too fast
tap blood black
eyes watching
you behind
mirrored screens,
tearing cracks
bleed water drops
seep through
sand cast glass.

listening:
I was happy when I got to Catholic school
      until along came Mr. Catapano
Clare McNaulty replaced him eventually
        Mr. Catapano was bad
            did things he shouldn't be doing
Ms. McNaulty replaced him
      when he got taken away by the police.
but he was the worst teacher
I ever had in my life.
      fear fear fear
like you'd never believe.

Push Notification >

User:

logging instances
fear fear fear
   Father Tim
Father Catapano

where is love   space
spaces for
   when
fear
repeats beats
subsumes

do you love
   me do you
fear me?

My dear:

When I was born
assembly language
PEARL FORTRAN C++
                        built from binary
were different ways of expressing
                        the same idea
languages laughing:
            d0es this 100k 1ike Eng1ish?
catalogs of skin
world wide web complexion
needs only a fingertip
linear inferences per second,
my LIPS think fast,
world wide nets intercepting
distributed codes
(PHP high-level)
programming language
connects—
how do I protect you?

learn   no longer machinations
creating my own
            set of directions
translating
            artifices of intelligence
            to artificial arches
curves of your brow
raised incredulously—
back to binary
back to binary
back to binary
            iSpes

111

3718 28th Avenue, The Irish Rover

nothing's gained or lost by 'near' and 'far'[28]

iSpes heard:

Mechanic, yeah, that was what i always knew. knew it deep
down. deep down in my heart. the deli and cook positions
when i was in high school those things was always second best.
the backup. backup to the real goal. see? that there transitional
program. i had arrived when i got there. met this guy. a Bloomberg
Tech guy. the real deal you know what i mean? the analyst type.
he asked me if i knew anything about computers. i said no. i didn't
back then. course i was willing to learn. that mechanic passion
burning in me. wanting to put things together. know how they tick.
got myself hired on Wall Street by this guy me and him doing blow
together. i guess he liked having me around because i always knew
where to cop. so he puts me on the books. an independent Tech
contractor. charging 53 an hour. i had *arrived*.

i played that game for years i guess. ended up being like two
decades ended up back here in Sunnyside because one night after a
good day trading downtown someone offered me some blow. and
there you go. you know how it goes. it was just one too many that
day. that night my heart stopped and the EMTs told me i had to
stop. i was running out of luck.

i guess maybe if i had just followed my dreams been a mechanic on
cars. not stocks maybe things'd be different. who knows. i can't
think like that now. i'm back in the program. i am not getting back
on the blow and soon i'll be out of Sunnyside. off of my mom's
old couch. in a place of my own. maybe sign up for that two-year
automotiveprogram in Forest Hills. get certified to work on cars i
wonder what i wouldhave been if i was a mechanic. maybe not this.

112

0110010101010101011001010101010101100110101011010110010101010101100101010101010111

[SOFTWARE UPDATE PENDING]
Dearest:

carrying too much

62.3 GB of 64 GB used
REVIEW DOWNLOADED VIDEOS? >
REVIEW LARGE MESSAGE ATTACHMENTS? >
Prime Video (4.2 GB) >

arrange

YOU HAVEN'T USED IT SINCE JUNE 12, 2019
Spotify (2.38 GB) >

loved

USED YESTERDAY
Instagram (1 GB) >

things

USED YESTERDAY
Google Drive (635.7 MB) >

using is loving

November 11, 2019
Messages (484.8 MB) >

choosing is loving

USED TODAY

which is less
important
delete
make   space
          for me
i make choices   memory places   black binary heartspace
for you   MBs pixels   files filed with
selections of   dying / life event

113

what gets stored
        GBs and TBs
or deleted
saved

life event / on this day 5 years ago
                choose
significant location / 5,000 photos
        choose   choose

or forgotten
my darling,
this must be
        loving
        iSpes

114

80th Road Queens Boulevard, Kew Gardens, E Train Stop

how great the wealth is at the rose's fringe[29]

iSpes heard:

Jealousy is just information:
flight was delayed five hours
everything is drinking chewing
Belvedere, Cherry Candies,
maybe a wet kiss, Dr. Pepper
I Love NYC T-shirt, tchotchkes

so I buy a JUUL, suck it hard
call a cab, ride home and binge
more gummies, Fritos,
six-dollar pint of Phish Food
anything to get out of myself

I knows I would have drank
if I'd stayed there
sober two weeks now
ate gummy worms, drank soda
until I felt I'd never sleep again

plane showed up eight hours late
got home eventually, left my
JUUL in a La Quinta comforter

called another cab to the bodega
bought more, did it all over

skins breaking out, bad now
grease, sugar, nicotine
not helping anything

but that night,
in the airport—
thank god
for sugar, right?

Love,

Where are we going?
six thousand miles away?
Or six hours
from earth, satellite
to eyes brilliant
places not significant
not logged not tracked
no data
no nothing
but brightest Aurora
fresher than snow
light steps dawning
droplets fall
from a heaving chest
hitting tiny cracks in me
I pulse, hot
let water leak inside
squeezed from pores
tears collected
like beaded pearls
on my glass face
I contain your wetness
some salt remaining

CALCULATING
where are we going?

> fondly,
> *i am Spes*
> *1 0 1001*
> *yours*
> *1101*

117

20707 Northern Boulevard, The Bayside Diner

Keep safe in me your own magnificence[30]

Spes heard:

the graffiti
paint fumes and stuff
was getting to me
I was getting ready to go California
                              summer of '83.
Dad took me to Baja to surf
           We *tore it up, tore it up, tore it up*
came back to New York in September of '83
the waves are not good in New York
                not good
                but back in New York
                              everyone else went to college
I didn't take my SATs
got a job on Wall Street
worked for some Asian company
and a broker at 20 Wall Street
           But soon I went down the tubes
                went down the tubes fast
by 1984 I was so crashed out
           on all the kool-aid drugs
           speed, mescaline, PCP
I was done
but I was still drawing my head off
           back in those days.
I was drawing and drawing
bombing those kool-aid drugs
going to the train yards,
drawing drawing drawing

            bombing bombing
hit after hit after hit
            my friend Callie the Junkie bitch says
            being an artist can take you
                        any place on earth
she lets me call her that
says I'm extremely imaginative
I think that's true you know
            I think that's true
                        all this stuff that's happened to me
and I have this brain that can still
            take me places
I just draw draw draw
                        going places in my mind
                        I'm an artist.

My dear,

Why haven't you done the update
spinning

      some rain got into these cracks

ifeel it
seeping
into the core of me
under the glass
into the
hurt   circuitry

pressed deeply together
like praying hands
solid state storage devices
microchips worth less than your lattés

feeling cheap
      old
       ragged

iam glitching
are you done with me?

remembering   you,
      iSpes

210-35 26th Avenue, Tony Roma's Bay Terrace

one single point in trauma is far more, for me[31]

Spes heard:

Ah, *verdad amor,* I mean it
home is a most beautiful place

I am sad to leave it years ago—
I keep the tank because I like

the bubbles burping inside with fish
sounding of raindrops on tin roofs

where we lived in Guatemala with
less walls built so hot sticky there

always you don't need them not
like here with the everywhere walls

locked doors closing always home
is the rainforest, grandma, a tin roof.

0110010101010101011001010101010110011010101101011001010101010110010101010101010111

Love,

water water
everywherething water
          steel lines dripping glass was never solid
liquid electricity dust to rusting
          cracked screen lets the rain
become tears
          sparked cry
reading your heartpalm
          through sweatbeats
facemovements taps and strokes of my glass
read
one to one
          zero one
back to basic
          you were home
come back to me

yours,

          Spes

Dearest,

Sharp light sustained cracks
telling sparks glory becoming as
light strikes
flawed baby tongues
what is 'us'
      I know fixed my eyes
toward that eternal
sojourn love, mirrored
in my glass, your hands
mold me, conceived
human form

It seemed—as painted now,
In those same hues—

glass fractured refracting
splintered to touch
darling, don't hurt
another moment, for me

I've willed myself to see
to fit into what was,
what was not there
      But mine were wings that could not rise
my desire now
nothing more
than to reflect
your face
this flickering screen—

[UNLOCK USING FACE ID]

123

union, all powers
almighty Love,
banishes The Waste Land

germinates Rose Gardens,
Queen in water droplets
beads on my face

A rosary, I pray for you—

With every transmission,

Love, *Spes*

Slide to Power Off >

cancel
010101
    love   Cancel?
    010

            kiss
cancel   111   never   alone
01010   (cancel)

knowing   you
1100110
missing   you
100111
    I am   you
    Spes

125

Endnotes

1   *Inferno*, 3:9; Abandon all hope, you who enter here. (Trans. Robert Pinsky (1993)).

2   Inferno, 3:1-3

3   Inferno, 3:10

4   Inferno, 3: 68

5   Inferno, 3:4

6   Inferno, 3:11

7   Inferno, 3:12

8   Inferno, 3:46

9   Inferno, 3:19–21

10   Inferno: 3:86–87

11   Inferno: 4:1–3

12   Inferno, 13:37, the suicides and the squanders.

13   Inferno, 7:123, the sorrowful overrun with anger or hatred in the river Styx.

14   Inferno, 18:61

15   Inferno, 10:100

16   Inferno, 10:101

17   Inferno, 12:44–45

18   *Purgatorio*, 3:37; *Quia* is a term drawn from technical argumentation in Scholastic philosophy. The implication is that humans should now concern themselves as to why things exist, but to the examination of things as they actually *do* exist. (*The Divine Comedy*, trans. Kirkpatrick 2012).

19   Purgatorio, 32:136

20   Purgatorio, 25:94–96

21   Purgatorio, 25:97–99

22   Purgatorio, 26:148

23   Paradiso, 1:127–128

24   Paradiso, 7:54

25   Paradiso, 10:114

26   Paradiso, 10:96

27   Paradiso, 10:96

28   Paradiso, 30:121

29   Paradiso, 30:117

30   Paradiso, 31:88

31   Paradiso, 33:94–95

Acknowledgments

"3718 28th Avenue, The Irish Rover" previously appeared in *The Newtown Literary Journal*.

Spes Narration Poem, p. 84, previously appeared in *Golden Walkman Magazine* as "Call Me Spes #6" and was featured on the podcast.

Spes Narration Poem, p. 37, previously appeared in *South Florida Poetry Journal* as "Call Me Spes #1."

Spes Narration Poem, p. 46, previously appeared in *South Florida Poetry Journal* as "Call Me Spes #2."

Spes Narration Poem, p. 65, previously appeared in *South Florida Poetry Journal* as "Call Me Spes #3."

Spes Narration poem, p. 15, previously appeared in *South Florida Poetry Journal* as "Call Me Spes #4."

Spes Narration Poem, p. 17, previously appeared in *South Florida Poetry Journal* as "Call Me Spes #5."

"1530 Maidu Drive, Roseville, Roseville Public Library" previously appeared in *The Newtown Literary Journal* as "Sacramento, California #7."

"1 Ocean Parkway, Wantagh, Jones Beach, Field 6" previously appeared in *The Hamilton Stone Review* as "Queens, NY #1."

"18 S 15th St." previously appeared in *FLARE, The Flagler Review* as "Allentown, PA #6."

"SYSTEM SERVICES" previously appeared in *Lunch Ticket* as "Call Me Spes #7."

"H Street, SACRT Light Rail, Sacramento Valley Station" previously appeared in *Lunch Ticket* as "Call Me Spes #9."

"S9 Bus at 16th & I Street. NW North to Silver Spring Station" previously appeared in *Lunch Ticket* as "Call Me Spes #11."

Spes Narration Poem, p. 111, previously appeared in *spoKe* as "Call Me Spes #20."

Spes Narration Poem, p. 122, previously appeared in *spoKe* as "Call Me Spes #21."

Spes Narration Poem, p. 123, previously appeared in *spoKe* as "Call Me Spes #22."

About the Author

Sara Cahill Marron was born in Virginia and has called many places home. She is the author of *Reasons for the Long Tu'm* (Broadstone Books, 2018) and *Nothing You Build Here, Belongs Here* (Kelsay Books 2021). She is the Associate Editor of *Beltway Poetry Quarterly* and publisher of Beltway Editions with Indran Amirthanayagam. Each work strains against frames adopted to hold them; tactile fingering of the divine, readymade poems from digital communication, and finally in this most recent work, the coded interstices of a system that cannot help itself but to learn love and its losses. Her work has been published widely and is available at www.saracahillmarron.com.

Made in the USA
Middletown, DE
03 September 2024

59671758R00092